WHAT THE BIBLE SAYS®

The Marriage Supper of the Lamb

The Battle of Armageddon

What the Bible Says:

The Marriage Supper of the Lamb/The Battle of Armageddon

Published by: Armor Books
P. O. Box 1050
Lawrenceville, GA 30045
Web Site: http://www.armorbooks.com
All rights reserved.

This is a derivative writing taken from the collective works of the late Finis Jennings Dake, and used by permission of the copyright holders. Unless otherwise noted, all Scripture quotations are from the Holy Bible, King James Version

Copyright © 2003 by Armor Books
First Printing 2003
Printed in the United States of America.
ISBN: 1-55829-081-8 (paperback)

01 02 03 04 05   87654321

CONTENTS

CONTENTS (CONTINUED)

PREFACE

For many Christians, the Bible is a book of mystery, full of hidden meaning only to be understood by pastors and seminarians who have devoted lifetimes to uncovering the truths found within its pages. Latin was the language of the Bible for centuries, and many still approach the Scriptures as if they were written in a foreign tongue. A few stories are learned in Sunday School, a handful of popular verses memorized, but many Christians fear to turn the pages of their Bibles into unfamiliar territory.

But there is no reason to be afraid. The Bible is the easiest book in the world to understand. You don't need to be a pastor or have a seminary degree. God designed the Bible to be understood by you and me, and the truths He intended for us to learn are easily found within its pages.

The "*What the Bible Says*" booklets are designed to illustrate simple biblical truths on topics that many consider to be particularly difficult to grasp. This book strives to let the Bible speak for itself, and therefore, a comprehensive list of scripture references for each of the topics discussed will be presented. Although it's not necessary to look up each and every reference in order to understand what the Bible is saying on a particular topic, we'll focus on the primary references, and provide a thorough list of supporting scriptures for you to study on your own.

HOW TO UNDERSTAND THE BIBLE

Here's the most important rule to follow when studying the Bible: You must take the Bible literally wherever it is at all possible. Obviously, there are times when the language of the Bible cannot be taken literally, and then we know it is to be understood figuratively. When this is the case, it is our job to find the literal truth conveyed by the figurative language, just as if it were expressed in literal language without the use of figures. For more on this topic, see the Appendix, "Biblical Studies."

FIGURATIVE LANGUAGE OF THE BIBLE

The Bible contains some figurative language. A lot of confusion is caused when literal passages of scripture are mistakenly understood figuratively, and the same holds true for scripture that is interpreted as literal, when it is obviously figurative in nature. So, what is figurative language in the Bible? How can we recognize it when we find it? Simply put, figurative language, or a "figure of speech" occurs when we use words in a different sense from that which is ordinarily given them. Figures of speech are used to give emphasis and to add attraction and variety to human expression. It is important to note that they are never used for the purpose of doing away with literal truth. Instead, figures of speech set forth literal truth in another form than that in which it could be literally expressed. What we're looking for is the literal truth found in the figurative language. Above all, we must not permit figures of speech to do away with the intended truth. If we fail to understand the literal truth expressed by the figure of speech, then it has failed in its purpose.

Now that we understand figures of speech, how can we tell whether a particular statement is intended to be understood literally or figuratively? It's easy! There's a fundamental rule to keep in mind when determining whether the language is literal or figurative: Every statement in the Bible is to be understood literally, when at all possible, and where it is clear that it is literal;

> *Above all, we must not permit figures of speech to do away with the intended truth. If we fail to understand the literal truth expressed by the figure of speech, then it has failed in its purpose.*

otherwise, it is figurative. In other words, what cannot be literal must be figurative. The subject matter itself will always make this clear.

There are two kinds of figures of speech we find in the Bible: first, there are those involving only a word, as in Galatians 2:9 where Peter, James, and John are called "pillars" of the Church; second, there are those involving a thought expressed in several words or sentences, such as the parable, allegory, symbol, type, riddle, fable, and enigma.

GOD'S PROMISES ARE ESPECIALLY SIMPLE

We've stated that many people think the Bible is hard to understand. In particular, this belief is held by many concerning the prophecies, the proverbs, and some figures of speech. However, these seemingly difficult parts of the Bible are no more difficult to understand than the sections of the Bible that deal with history, or those that many consider to be "simple." Prophecy is nothing more than history written beforehand and should be understood in this light. All riddles, allegories, types, symbols, and figures of speech are either explained in Scripture, or are clear in themselves as to their true meaning.

When it comes to the promises of God, there shouldn't be any misunderstanding about what they say or mean. Every promise of God is a simple statement of obligation to

9

men that God will give them certain benefits when they meet certain conditions. All the promises of God are conditional, as can be seen in the Scriptures themselves. If you want to receive the promised benefits, you must accept the promise for what it says and meet the conditions required. You can then depend upon the fulfillment of God's promise *in this life*. Since God cannot lie, man is assured that what God has promised He is abundantly able to perform. None of God's promises need further interpretation. All that we must do is act upon what the Bible says and believe that God's promise will be fulfilled in our lives. Do not attach any other conditions to God's promises than what is plainly written. When the conditions are met the blessings will be realized. As the Apostle Paul writes in 2 Corinthians 1:20, "For ALL the promises of God in Him are yea, and in Him Amen, unto the glory of God by us."

Chapter One

THE MARRIAGE SUPPER

Let us rejoice and be glad and give the glory to Him, for the marriage of the Lamb has come and His bride has made herself ready (Rev. 19:7)

Then he said to me, "Write, 'Blessed are those who are invited to the marriage supper of the Lamb.'" And he said to me, "These are true words of God" (Rev. 19:9)

The marriage supper of the Lamb is mentioned only in Revelation 19:7 and 9. Everything we know about this event is revealed in these two verses. Some use Psalm 45 and Matthew 22; 25:1-13 for additional information relating to this event, but there is no definite connection between these scriptures and the Revelation 19 passage.

That the Church is now married to Christ is clear from many passages in the Bible. The eight proofs listed below are but a few of the arguments proving this union:

1. Jesus called Himself the bridegroom:

> And Jesus said unto them, Can the children of the bridechamber mourn, as long as the bridegroom is with them? but the days will come, when the bridegroom shall be taken from them, and then shall they fast (Mt. 9:15; cf. Mk. 2:19-20; Lk. 5:34-35).

2. John called Christ the bridegroom. The Greek word for "bridegroom" in all these passages is *numphios*, "a newly married man:"

> He that hath the bride is the bridegroom: but the friend of the bridegroom, which standeth and heareth him, rejoiceth greatly because of the bridegroom's voice: this my joy therefore is fulfilled (Jn. 3:29)

3. Christians are married to God and Christ under the terms of the New Testament as Israel was married to God under the terms of the Old Testament:

> And to Jesus the mediator of the new covenant, and to the blood of sprinkling, that speaketh better things than that of Abel (Heb. 12:24; cf. Mt. 26:28; Lk. 22:20; 2 Cor. 3; Heb. 12:24)

4. Paul taught that Christians are now married to Christ by the terms of the New Covenant:

> Wherefore, my brethren, ye also are become dead to the law by the body of Christ; that ye should be married to another, even to him who is raised from the dead, that we should bring forth fruit unto God (Rom. 7:4)

5. Paul also taught that Old Testament saints will not be perfected apart from New Testament saints. What this means is that all will be perfected together as

those who comprise the inhabitants of the New Jerusalem, the Lamb's wife:

> God having provided some better thing for us, that they without us should not be made perfect (Heb. 11:40)

6. Jesus, after the ascension, recognized that believers on earth were already His bride or were to be a part of His bride:

> I Jesus have sent mine angel to testify unto you these things in the churches. I am the root and the offspring of David, and the bright and morning star. And the Spirit and the bride say, Come. And let him that heareth say, Come. And let him that is athirst come. And whosoever will, let him take the water of life freely (Rev. 22:16-17)

7. Paul used the marriage relationship to illustrate and teach the relationship of Christ to His Church, proving Christians are now married to Christ:

But I would have you know, that
the head of every man is Christ;
and the head of the woman is
the man; and the head of Christ
is God (1 Cor. 11:3)

8. Paul taught that believers are now
joined to the Lord or married to Him
in one Spirit, as Israel was in the Old
Testament days:

They shall ask the way to Zion
with their faces thitherward,
saying, Come, and let us join
ourselves to the LORD in a per-
petual covenant that shall not be
forgotten (Jer. 50:5)

The Marriage of Christ

Christians are now married to Christ. The
fact is evident from the scripture references
we've just studied. However, we see in
Revelation 19:1-10 that although this union
between Christ and His Church is formally
acknowledged, there are still final marriage
festivities yet to come. The seeming differ-

15

ence may be explained by Hebrew custom. For example, we have Mary's espousal to Joseph recorded in Matthew's Gospel:

> Now the birth of Jesus Christ was on this wise: When as his mother Mary was espoused to Joseph, before they came together, she was found with child of the Holy Ghost (Mt. 1:18)

According to Hebrew custom, the betrothed parties were legally in the position of a married couple following their "espousal" or engagement. Any unfaithfulness in this period was considered adultery (Dt. 22:23; Mt. 1:19). The concluding festivities took place at the actual time of coming together as man and wife at which time a marriage supper was given. The marriage was consummated by entrance into the wedding chamber. The marriage supper of the Lamb in Revelation 19 is simply the concluding ceremony, not the marriage contract entered into at conversion.

A Parenthetical Passage

This passage (Rev. 19:1-10) is generally taken to be parenthetical, a break in what is otherwise a continuous narrative. Although we find the account of the marriage supper ocurring in sequence after the vial judgments, it will be literally fulfilled later, in Heaven, when all the tribulation saints and the two witnesses are raptured at the end of the Week. The return of Christ will take place during the events mentioned during the seventh vial, or soon thereafter, but the marriage supper will take place before He comes. Because of this, we know Revelation

> *Although we find the account of the marriage supper occurring in sequence after the vial judgments, it will be literally fulfilled later, in Heaven, when all the tribulation saints and the two witnesses are raptured at the end of the Week.*

19:1-10 *must* be parenthetical, as it explains what takes place in Heaven just before Christ comes back to the earth with the saints. It is clear that the multitudes in Heaven in this passage will be giving glory to God because He has already judged the "great whore" (mentioned in Rev. 19:2) and the smoke of the destruction of Literal Babylon is at that time ascending up.

This "great whore" could not be the same as the woman in Revelation 17, for she will have been destroyed 3½ years before the fulfillment of this passage and her smoke would not be ascending at this time. This judgment will be from God Himself, who will have avenged the blood of His servants at her hand. Hence, this rejoicing is in direct obedience to the command of Revelation 18:20, calling all of "heaven, and ye saints, and ye apostles, and ye prophets" to rejoice over her judgment. Her smoke is to ascend to God "for ever and ever," a term that is used fourteen times in this

> *This judgment will be from God Himself, who will have avenged the blood of His servants at her hand. Hence, this rejoicing is in obedience to the command of Revelation 18:20, calling all of "heaven, and ye saints, and ye apostles, and ye prophets" to rejoice over her judgment.*

book. This corresponds to the eternal desolations of Literal Babylon described in Isaiah 13:19-22 and in Jeremiah 50:13, 23, 39-40; 51:26, 37, 62. This may be the one place where the eternal Lake of Fire will be visible to the earth–dwellers living in the New Earth after the Millennium (Isa. 66:22-24; Rev. 14: 9-11).

Next, we have mention in this passage of the elders and living creatures worshipping God. This is the last time they are seen in Revelation. Then a voice from the throne says, "Praise our God, all ye his servants, and ye that fear him, both small and great." John then hears the voice of a great multitude as the sound of many waters and powerful thunderings saying, "Alleluia: for the Lord God omnipotent reigneth." Finally, the angel shows John the marriage supper of the Lamb.

The statement in Revelation 19:7, "His wife hath made herself ready," shows that there are certain preparations to make in order to be ready. This seems clear from her white

19

robe which is the righteousness of the saints (Rev. 19:8). It is impossible to describe the wedding supper, since we have no description given of this event. All we know about it is that it will be a real banquet—this is not a metaphor or figurative representation.

The Greek word for *marriage* means "marriage feast" proving that the supper will be as literal and as real as any we may have experienced here on earth (cf. Rev. 19:1-10 with Mt. 22:2; 25:10). The magnitude of such a wedding supper need not disturb the reader for "with God all things are possible." If we can conceive of thousands eating at an earthly banquet, we can certainly understand how innumerable companies will do so in Heaven. That food will be eaten in Heaven is clear from Lk. 22:16, 18, 30; Rev. 2:7, 17; 22:1-2; Ps.78:25; Ex. 24:11.

When John saw these things, he fell down to worship the angel as he would worship God, but was immediately restrained from doing so, and was told that he (the angel) was also a redeemed person and a fellow–servant of the brethren the prophets, and of those who have the testimony of Jesus, which is the spirit of prophecy.

Two Suppers in Revelation 19

The marriage supper of the Lamb, which is discussed in the first chapters of Revelation 19, is not to be confused with the "supper of the great God," recorded in the last part of the chapter:

> And I saw an angel standing in the sun; and he cried with a loud voice, saying to all the fowls that fly in the midst of heaven, Come and gather yourselves together unto the supper of the great God; That ye may eat the flesh of kings, and the flesh of captains, and the flesh of mighty men, and the flesh of horses, and of them that sit on them, and the flesh of all men, both free and bond, both small and great (Rev. 19:17-18)

Whereas the marriage supper of the Lamb is the beautiful culmination of the an event that begins at conversion, the "supper of the great God" follows directly behind a terrible event—the final doom of all who have opposed God. The "supper" is the cleansing of the earth from the greatest battle of them all—Armageddon, the final battle between righteousness and evil.

Chapter Two

The Supper of the Great God

This title, "the supper of the great God," is found in Revelation 19:17. Earlier, in Revelation 16:14, Armageddon is called "the battle of that great day of God Almighty." The supper will be closely related to the Second Coming of Christ and will be necessary to cleanse the land of all refuse from the Battle of Armageddon. The need of cleansing the land will be so great that the animal and fowl creations will be called upon to assist. Note the following points which are so clear in themselves that we shall simply quote the verses applicable to each point and give corresponding references to each passage.

The Invited Guests

"And I saw an angel standing in the sun; and he cried with a loud voice, saying to all

the fowls that fly in the midst of heaven,
Come and gather yourselves together unto
the supper of the great God" (Rev. 19:17;
Ezek. 39:17-23; Mt. 24:28, 40-42; Lk. 17:
34-37).

The Supper Foretold

"That ye may eat the flesh of kings, and
the flesh of captains, and the flesh of mighty
men, and the flesh of horses, and of them that
sit on them, and the flesh of all men, both
free and bond, both small and great" (Rev.
19:18; Isa. 34:3; Ezek. 39:17-23; Mt. 24:28;
Lk. 17:37).

The Supper Gathered

"And I saw the beast and the kings of the
earth, and their armies, gathered together to
make war against him that sat on the horse,
and against his army" (Rev. 19:19; 14:14-20;
16:13-16; 17:14; Ezek. 38–39; Joel 3; Zech.
14; 2 Thess. 1:7-9; Jude 14; Isa. 63:1-5).

The Supper Slain and Prepared

"And the beast was taken, and with him the false prophet that wrought miracles before him, with which he had deceived them that received the mark of the Beast and them that worshipped his image. These both were cast alive into a Lake of Fire burning with brimstone. And the remnant were slain with the sword of him that sat upon the horse, which sword proceeded out of his mouth" (Rev. 19:20-21a; Isa. 34:63; Ezek. 38-39; Joel 3; Zech. 14; Rev. 14:14-20).

The Supper Eaten

"And all the fowls were filled with their flesh" (Rev. 19:2lb; Ezek. 39:4, 17-23; Mt. 24:28; Lk. 17:37).

The Battle

Preceeding the "supper of the great God" will be a great battle—Armageddon. The idea that Armageddon must be fought between nations as is common war is wrong. When the last two world wars broke out, some of the dailies printed flaming headlines reading "Armageddon!" or "Is it Armageddon?" All such musings in the hearts of men show a failure to discern the times in which we live and what prophecy has to say on the subject. To answer any question about Armageddon, We must consult the Bible, for Armageddon is exclusively a Bible theme. Armageddon is to follow the fulfillment of all the Revelation recorded down through chapter 19. We'll look more closely at this battle in the following chapter.

Chapter Three

THE BATTLE OF ARMAGEDDON

Where Armageddon Will Be Fought

And I saw three unclean spirits
like frogs come out of the mouth
of the dragon, and out of the
mouth of the beast, and out of
the mouth of the false prophet.
For they are the spirits of devils,
working miracles, which go forth
unto the kings of the earth and of
the whole world, to gather them
to the battle of that great day of
God Almighty. Behold, I come as
a thief. Blessed is he that watch-
eth, and keepeth his garments,
lest he walk naked, and they see
his shame. And he gathered them
together into a place called in
the Hebrew tongue Armageddon
(Rev. 16:13-16)

The word "Armageddon" occurs only once in Scripture. It is the name of a place where the greatest battle of all times will be fought. The battle itself however, under different terms, is mentioned many times in Scripture. The battleground is a place where the three unclean spirits will gather the nations together to battle (Rev. 16:13-16). Armageddon is called "the valley of Jehoshaphat" in other places in the Bible, which identifies the location of the battle as a place extending from Mount Carmel southeast to Jerusalem (Joel 3).

The word "Armageddon" is derived from two Hebrew words, *har*, meaning "a mountain or range of hills," "hill country," and *Megiddo*, meaning "rendezvous." The two words put together (Har–Megiddo) refer to the Hill of Megiddo on the south side of the valley of Megiddo or Esdraelon southeast of Mount Carmel (2 Chr. 35:22; Zech. 12:11). "Megiddo" was the capital of a portion of Canaan that fell to Joshua (Josh. 12:21; 17: 11; Judg. 1:27). It is at the entrance to a pass across the Carmel mountain range, on the main highway between Asia and Africa, and is the key position between the Euphrates and the Nile. It has been a battlefield of many peoples throughout many ages. Thothmes III, the founder of the old Egyptian Empire, said, "Megiddo is worth a thousand cities."

This place will possibly be the headquarters of the Antichrist when he comes down from the north, after having conquered Russia and the countries north and east of the old Roman Empire. Revelation 16:13-16 says, "And he gathered them together into a place called in the Hebrew tongue Armageddon." There he

> *"Megiddo" was the capital of a portion of Canaan that fell to Joshua. It is the key position between the Euphrates and the Nile. It has been a battlefield of many peoples throughout many ages. Thothmes III, the founder of the old Egyptian Empire, said, "Megiddo is worth a thousand cities."*

will await the return of Christ, who is expected to come from Heaven to set His feet on the Mount of Olives and deliver Israel when half of the city of Jerusalem is taken (Zech. 14:1-5). The devil "knoweth that he hath but a short time" (Rev. 12:12) and it will be common knowledge to the Antichrist and others that Christ is expected at the end of the 1,260 days of Revelation 11:1-3; 12:6, 14; 13:5.

By some means, the Antichrist will have lost his control of Jerusalem toward the last part of the Week. He will have been personally directing his armies against the countries of the north and east (Dan. 11:44) and the Jews, in his absence, will gain control of the city again and will be in possession of Jerusalem at the time the Antichrist comes down from the north to destroy them. The two witnesses will have a hand in helping the remnant of Israel obtain control of the city by use of the miracles they will be able to perform. At any rate, it is clear from Zechariah 14 that the Antichrist comes back from the north and

> *The Antichrist will have been personally directing his armies against the countries of the north and east (Dan. 11:44) and the Jews, in his absence, will gain control of the city again and will be in possession at the time Antichrist comes down from the north to destroy them.*

gathers the nations to do battle against the Jews and the inhabitants of Jerusalem by the time Christ comes back to the earth.

The Antichrist is not from Russia

> Therefore, thou son of man, prophesy against Gog, and say, Thus saith the Lord GOD; Behold, I am against thee, O Gog, the chief prince of Meshech and Tubal: And I will turn thee back, and leave but the sixth part of thee, and will cause thee to come up from the north parts, and will bring thee upon the mountains of Israel: And I will smite thy bow out of thy left hand, and will cause thine arrows to fall out of thy right hand. Thou shalt fall upon the mountains of Israel, thou, and all thy bands, and the people that is with thee: I will give thee unto the ravenous birds of every sort, and to the beasts of the field to be devoured (Ezek. 39:1-4)

31

Ezekiel 38 and 39 are also clear that after the Antichrist conquers Russia, Germany, and the other countries north and east of his empire, he will then return from the north with his armies, and those of these newly conquered countries, to destroy Israel and stop Christ from setting up His kingdom. These chapters in Ezekiel are generally interpreted as proving that the Antichrist will come from Russia because he is "the chief prince of Meshech and Tubal," who will lead Russia

> *The Anitchrist becomes the "chief prince of Mescheck and Tubal" by conquering these lands, and not by birth. Daniel 11:44 proves that the Antichrist first conquers these countries of the north and east before he can be their chief prince and lead them down against the Jews.*

and Germany and others down from the north into Palestine. However, such is not the case. The Anitchrist becomes the "chief prince of Mescheck and Tubal" by conquering these lands, and not by birth. Daniel 11:44 proves that the Antichrist first conquers these countries of the north and east before he can be their chief prince and lead them down against the Jews.

The Time Armageddon Will Be Fought

1. Armageddon will be fought when Israel will be safe in the wilderness and "Sheba, and Dedan, and the merchants of Tarshish, with all the young lions thereof [called Edom, Moab, chief of the children of Ammon, including all the Arabian chiefs of the Arabian peninsula, Dan. 11:41; Rev. 12:6, 14-17], shall say to thee, Art thou come to take a spoil? . . . to carry away silver and gold, to take away cattle and goods, to take a great spoil?" (Ezek. 38:1-16).
2. It will be fought when Antichrist has completed his conquest of Russia, Germany, and the other countries north and east of his ten-kingdom empire (Dan. 11:44; Ezek. 38:1-16).
3. It will be at the Second Coming of Christ in order to deliver the Jews and Jerusalem from the armies of the

33

Antichrist (Joel 3; Zech. 14; Isa. 63:
1-6; Jude 14; 2 Thess. 1:7-10).

4. It will be imme-
diately after the
Tribulation (Mt. 24:
29-31; 25:31-46).

5. It will be after the
marriage supper of
the Lamb (Rev. 19:
1-21).

6. It will be at the time
Satan is bound for
one thousand years
(Rev. 19:11; 20:3).

> *The Battle of
> Armageddon will not
> be an ordinary battle
> between two sets of
> earthly nations, as
> some teach. It will
> be a battle between
> the armies of Heaven
> under Christ and the
> armies of the earth
> under the Dragon,
> the Beast, and False
> Prophet.*

7. It will be at the time when Jerusalem is
surrounded by the armies of the nations
and half of the city is taken (Zech. 14:
1-15: Rev. 14:14-21; 16:13-16).

8. It will be just before the Millennium
(Rev. 19:11–20:3).

9. It will be at the end of this age (Mt. 13:
40-43, 25:31-46).

10. It will be at the time God sets up His
kingdom on the earth (Dan. 2:44; 7:13-
14, 18-27).

11. It will be when the first resurrection has been completed (Rev. 19:11–20:6).
12. It will be at the end of Daniel's Seventieth Week (Dan. 9:27; Rev. 13:5; 19:11-21).
13. It will be forty-two months after Antichrist is given power over the ten kingdoms (Rev. 13:5; 19:11-21).
14. It will take place when men will think there will be universal peace because Antichrist will have conquered much of the world (1 Thess. 5:1-3).
15. It will be at the beginning of the "day of the Lord" (2 Thess. 2:1-12; 2 Thess. 5: 13; Rev. 19:11-21; 20:1-3).

The Combatants at Armageddon

The Battle of Armageddon will not be an ordinary battle between two sets of earthly nations, as some teach. It will be a battle between the armies of Heaven under Christ and the armies of the earth under the Dragon, the Beast, and False Prophet. On the side of Christ there will be earthly Israel (Zech. 14:1-

15), the angels of God (Mt. 25:31-45; 2 Thess. 1:7-10), and the resurrected saints of all ages (Zech. 14:1-5; Jude 14; Rev. 19:11-21). On the side of Antichrist there will be the devil and his angels and demons (Rev. 12:7-12; 16:13-16; Rev. 20:1-3), the ten kings (Rev. 17:14-17; Dan. 2:44; 7:19-27), the countries north and east of the ten kingdoms who will have been recently conquered by Antichrist (Dan. 11:44; Ezek. 38–39; Rev. 16:

The purpose of God will be to deliver Israel from total destruction by the Antichrist and the many nations under him, to punish these nations for persecution of the Jews, and to set up a kingdom on the earth with Christ as its head.

12), and many other nations that will co-operate with the Antichrist through the ministry of the three unclean frogs (Rev. 16:13-16; Zech. 14: 1-5, 16; Ezek. 38–39).

The Purpose of Armageddon

The purpose of God will be to deliver Israel from total destruction by the Antichrist and the many nations under him (Zech. 14;

Isa. 63:1-10), to punish these nations for persecution of the Jews (Mt. 25:31-46), to set up a kingdom on the earth with Christ as its head (Dan. 7:13-14; Lk. 1:32), to rid the earth of all rebellion and to restore God's dominion on earth as before the fall (1 Cor. 15:24-29; Eph. 1:10), to give man one more test before destroying every rebel on the earth (Eph. 1:10; Rev. 20:1-10), and to establish the eternal perfect state (Rev. 21:1–22:5; 2 Pet. 3:10-13). The purpose of man and Satan will be to stop God's plan in taking over the earthly governments, and to avert their own impending doom, should they be defeated (Rev. 12:12; 19:19-21; 20:1-10; Zech. 14:1-5).

The Length of the Battle of Armageddon

According to Zechariah 14:1-14, the battle will only be one day long:

> . . . the Lord my God shall come,
> and *all the saints with thee*. And
> it shall come to pass *in that day*,
> that the light shall not be clear, nor

dark: but it shall be *one day* which
shall be known to the Lord, not
day, nor night: but it shall come to
pass, that at evening time it shall
be light (Zech. 14:5b-6)

The Results of Armageddon

1. There will be total defeat of the armies
   of the earth and the spirit forces under
   Satan (Isa. 24:21–23; 25:7; 63:1-6; Rev.
   19:19–20:3; Ezek. 38–39).
2. All the vast armies of the nations will
   be destroyed except "the sixth part"
   (Ezek. 39:2; Rev. 19:19-21; Zech. 14:
   1-15: Joel 3).
3. These armies will make carcasses for
   the fowls of the heavens to eat for as
   long as seven months (Ezek. 39:4-24;
   Rev. 19:17-21; Mt. 24:27-28, 40-42;
   Lk. 17:34-37; Job 39:27-30).
4. The Beast and False Prophet will be cast
   into the Lake of Fire (Rev. 19:20; Dan. 7:
   11; 8:25; 11:45; 2 Thess. 2:8-9).
5. The devil and angels will be cast into

the bottomless pit (Rev. 20:1-7).

6. Blood will flow up to the horses' bridles (Rev. 14:14-21; Ezek. 39:17-24).

7. Israel will be delivered and vindicated and God's eternal kingdom will be set top (Mt. 25:31-46; Dan. 2:44; 7:18, 23-27; Rev. 11:15; 20:1-10; 21:2–22:5).

The Destruction of the Antichrist's Army:

1. By the brightness of Christ's coming (2 Thess. 2:8).

2. By angels (Mt. 24:27-31; 2 Thess. 1:7-10).

3. By the saints (Zech. 14:5; Jude 14; Rev. 17:14; 19:11-21).

4. By hail and rain from Heaven (Ezek. 38:22; Rev. 16:21).

5. By the Jews (Zech. 12:1–13:1; 14:14).

6. By the armies of the Beast slaying each other (Ezek. 38:21; Zech. 14:13).

7. By fire, brimstone, and pestilence from Heaven (Ezek. 38:22; 2 Thess. 1:7-10).

8. By a plague from God which will consume their flesh (Zech. 14:12).

9. By the rod and sword of Christ's mouth (Isa. 11:14; Rev. 19:15).

The Bottomless Pit or Abyss

The Abyss is the abode or prison of demons and certain angelic beings. No human being ever goes to the Abyss. The Old Testament equivalent is Abaddon and is translated "destruction" in Job 26:5-6; 28:22; 31:12; Ps. 88:11; Pr. 15:11; 27:30. In the New Testament the Greek word is *abussos*, and means Abyss, "an immeasurable depth." It is a very deep chasm in the lower parts of the earth. It is translated "deep" (Lk. 8:26-31; Rom.10:7) and "bottomless pit" (Rev. 9:1-3, 11; 11:7; 17:8; 20:1-10).

Chapter Four

ARMAGEDDON AND THE ANTICHRIST

The Beast out of the Sea

And I stood upon the sand of the sea, and saw a beast rise up out of the sea, having seven heads and ten horns, and upon his horns ten crowns, and upon his heads the name of blasphemy. And the beast which I saw was like unto a leopard, and his feet were as the feet of a bear, and his mouth as the mouth of a lion: and the dragon gave him his power, and his seat, and great authority. And I saw one of his heads as it were wounded to death; and his deadly wound was healed: and all the world wondered after the beast. And they worshipped the dragon which gave power unto

41

the beast: and they worshipped the beast, saying, Who is like unto the beast? who is able to make war with him? And there was given unto him a mouth speaking great things and blasphemies; and power was given unto him to continue forty and two months. And he opened his mouth in blasphemy against God, to blaspheme his name, and his tabernacle, and them that dwell in heaven. And it was given unto him to make war with the saints, and to overcome them: and power was given him over all kindreds, and tongues, and nations. And all that dwell upon the earth shall worship him, whose names are not written in the book of life of the Lamb slain from the foundation of the world. If any man have an ear, let him hear. He that leadeth into captivity shall go into captivity: he that killeth with the sword must be killed with the sword. Here is the patience and the faith of the saints. Here is wisdom. Let him that hath understanding count the number of the beast: for it is the number of a man; and his number is Six hundred threescore and six (Rev. 13:1-10, 18)

As we have seen, the battle at Armageddon will pit the the Antichrist and his forces against the armies of the Lord. In this chapter, we'll look more closely at what the Scriptures have to say about the Antichrist, his origin, rise to power, and eventual downfall.

The "beast" in Revelation refers to the rise of a kingdom and, more particularly, to the Antichrist, the earthly head of the kingdom. It also symbolizes a supernatural spirit out of the Abyss, as we shall later see. Beasts in Scripture symbolize kingdoms and kings (Dan. 2:38, 39; 7:2-7 with 7:17, 23), as well as supernatural powers which control the kingdoms. This passage is certainly not the only scripture referring to the Antichrist, but it is perhaps the most comprehensive, providing a wealth of detail about the person of the

Antichrist, as well as his rise to power. Let's take a look at what this passage has to tell us about this man.

Who is the Antichrist?

At the present time, this question can't be answered. Actually, the question is unanswerable and will remain so until the Antichrist personally makes a covenant with Israel for seven years (we'll take a look at this later—it's recorded in Dan. 9:27). Many in the past have speculated that it could be the pope, Stalin, Hitler, the United Nations, a variety of other tyrants from countries spanning the globe, numerous organizations and powerful world figures. A great deal of harm has been done to the subject of prophecy by this kind of speculation, and it has caused many to turn their backs on the possibility of prophetic inspiration when they have seen the uninspired results of this kind of "guessing game." The following points prove that no man now prominent in world affairs could possibly be the Antichrist.

From Where does the Antichrist Come?

We don't know who the Antichrist may be, but we do know where he will come from. The Scriptures are clear that the Antichrist *must* come from a particular geographic area. If we turn to the book of Daniel, we'll see how this is clearly illustrated.

> This image's head was of fine gold, his breast and his arms of silver, his belly and his thighs of brass, His legs of iron, his feet part of iron and part of clay. Thou sawest till that a stone was cut out without hands, which smote the image upon his feet that were of iron and clay, and brake them to pieces. Then was the iron, the clay, the brass, the silver, and the gold, broken to pieces together, and became like the chaff of the summer threshingfloors; and the wind carried them away, that no place was found for them: and the stone that smote the image became a

great mountain, and filled the whole earth (Dan. 2:32-35)

The first was like a lion, and had eagle's wings: I beheld till the wings thereof were plucked, and it was lifted up from the earth, and made stand upon the feet as a man, and a man's heart was given to it. As concerning the rest of the beasts, they had their dominion taken away: yet their lives were prolonged for a season and time. These great beasts, which are four, are four kings, which shall arise out of the earth (Dan. 7:4, 12, 17)

In Daniel 2 and 7 we have two visions that cover the world powers from Daniel's day to the Second Coming of Christ. The "head of gold" on the image (Dan. 2:32, 35, 38) and the "lion" (Dan. 7:4, 12, 17) symbolize Babylon, Nebuchadnezzar's kingdom. The "breast and arms of silver" on the image (Dan. 2:32, 35, 39) and the "bear" (Dan. 7:5, 12, 17) symbolize Medo–Persia, which followed Babylon in the punishment of Israel (Dan. 2:39; 5:24-31;

6:1-28; 8:1-4, 20; 10:1-20; 11:1-3; 2 Chr. 36: 22; Ezra 1:1-3). The "belly and thighs of brass" on the image (Dan. 2:39) and the "leopard" (Dan. 7:6, 12, 17) symbolize the old Grecian Empire of Alexander the Great that followed Medo–Persia in the times of the Gentiles (Dan. 2:39; 8:20-21; 11:1-4).

The "legs of iron" on the image (Dan. 2:33-35, 40) and the nondescript "beast" (Dan. 7:7-8, 17-27) symbolize the old Roman Empire that followed the Grecian Empire and its four divisions in the persecution of Israel. The "feet and toes" of iron and clay on the image (Dan. 2: 33-35, 41-44) and "the

> *The "feet and toes" of iron and clay on the image and "the ten horns" on the nondescript beast symbolize ten kings who will head ten separate governments from ten separate capitals inside the old Roman Empire in the days of the Second Coming of Christ.*

ten horns" on the nondescript beast (Dan. 7: 8, 20-24) symbolize ten kings who will head ten separate governments from ten separate capitals inside the old Roman Empire in the days of the Second Coming of Christ.

Some call these ten kingdoms the Revived Roman Empire, but to be technical, there is no such thing as the revival of the Roman Empire. This would require the old Roman territory to be formed into one empire again, to be ruled by one man from Rome—something the Bible doesn't teach. Instead, the Scriptures are clear that there will be ten kingdoms formed inside of this territory instead of one empire (Dan. 2:44; 7:23-24; Rev. 17:8-17). It would be best to call these ten kingdoms the "Revised Roman Empire" due to the fact that they will be formed inside the old Roman territory.

Daniel did not see a little toe growing out of the ten toes in Daniel 2, but in Daniel 7 he did see a "little horn" growing out of the ten horns, which plucked up three of the ten horns by the roots (Dan. 7:7-8). This is explained by Daniel:

> The fourth beast shall be the fourth kingdom upon the earth [the old Roman Empire, which followed Babylon, Medo–Persia, and Greece from Daniel's day

on], which shall be diverse from
all kingdoms . . . the ten horns
out of this kingdom are ten kings
that shall arise: and another shall
rise after them; and he shall be
diverse from the first [the ten],
and he shall subdue three kings
[of the ten] (Dan. 7:23-24)

This will give the Antichrist power over
four of the ten kings. The other six of the ten
will agree to give their power to this "little
horn," and he will then form the eighth kingdom of Revelation 17:8-17.

It is clear that this "little horn" arises "after"
the ten kingdoms are formed, not "before,"
and that he does not have anything to do
with the rise of the ten kingdoms. He does
not come until "after" they are fully formed
and exist for a "short space," (Dan. 7:8; Rev.
17:9-11). The "little horn" as well as the "ten
horns" are all future events, for in Revelation
13:1-8; 17:9-17 it is clear that the ten kings
give their power and kingdom to the Beast
for forty–two months, and together they will
fight against Christ at Armageddon.

In Daniel 8 we have a vision of a ram and an he–goat. The ram symbolizes Medo–Persia, the same as the silver in the image of Daniel 2 and the bear of Daniel 7. The he–goat symbolizes the Grecian Empire the same as the brass in the image of Daniel 2 and the leopard of Daniel 7. The he–goat had a notable horn between its eyes, which was broken off, and in its place grew four horns and "out of one of them came forth the little horn." The interpretation of these things is given as follows:

> The ram which thou sawest having two horns are the [two] kings of Media and Persia. And the rough goat is the king [kingdom] of Grecia: and the great horn that is between his eyes is the first king [Alexander the Great who founded the old Grecian Empire]. Now that being broken [Alexander having died], whereas four stood up for it [that is, four horns grew on the he–goat instead of the great horn], four kingdoms shall

stand up out of the nation [the Grecian Empire shall be divided into four kingdoms], but not in his [Alexander's] power. And in the latter time of their kingdom, when the transgressors are come to the full, a king of fierce countenance, and understanding dark sentences, shall stand up [that is, the little horn shall come out of one of these four divisions of Greece in the last days of the existence of these four kingdoms] . . . He shall also stand up against the Prince of princes [Jesus Christ]; but he shall be broken without hand" by Christ at His Second Advent (Dan. 8:20-25, emphasis added)

These four divisions of Greece would be known today as Greece, Turkey, Syria and Egypt. Four of Alexander's generals divided his empire after his death. Cassander took Greece and Macedon, Lysimachus took Asia Minor or present Turkey and Thrace, Seleucus took Syria and Babylonia, and Ptolemy took Egypt. (This can be verified by anyone who will get an ancient history and see the map of the old Grecian Empire and its four divisions after the death of Alexander).

In Daniel 8:9 it is definitely stated that "the little horn" will come from one of the four horns, "out of one of them came forth a little horn, which waxed exceeding great, toward the south (Egypt), and toward the east (Babylonia), and toward the pleasant land (Palestine)." This verse is interpreted in verse 23 as "in the latter time of their kingdom (the existence of Greece, Turkey, Syria, and Egypt), when the transgressors are come to the full, a king of fierce countenance, and understanding dark sentences, shall stand up" and fight against "the Prince of princes" at His Second Advent.

> *The purpose of Daniel 8 in relation to Daniel 7 is to narrow down the coming of the Antichrist geographically from the ten kingdoms of the future Revised Roman Empire to four of the ten kingdoms, and reveal that Antichrist will come from either Greece, Turkey, Syria or Egypt.*

The purpose of Daniel 8 in relation to Daniel 7 is to narrow down the coming of the Antichrist geographically from the ten kingdoms of the future Revised Roman Empire to four of the ten kingdoms, and reveal that Antichrist will come from either Greece, Turkey, Syria or Egypt.

If we didn't have the vision of Daniel 8, we would have a much broader range of countries from which to choose. The Antichrist could then come from England, Holland, Belgium, France, Switzerland, Spain, Portugal, Italy, Austria, Hungary, Yugoslavia, Albania, or some other part of the old Roman Empire outside of the four divisions of the Grecian Empire. However, since the verses in Daniel 8 narrow the territory down from the ten kingdoms of the Roman Empire to the four divisions of the Grecian Empire, we know he must come from either Greece, Turkey, Syria, or Egypt.

If the Antichrist is coming from either Greece, Turkey, Syria, or Egypt, then it is obvious that he cannot come from Italy (it couldn't have been Mussolini), the Vatican (it's not the pope), England, America, Germany, Russia, or any other country outside the boundaries of the ancient Grecian Empire.

The Antichrist will come from one of these four divisions of Greece and will overthrow the other three, thus reviving the Grecian Empire, which will become the eighth or leopard kingdom of Revelation 13: 1-18; 17:1-17.

The Antichrist, the King of the North

In Daniel 11 we have a vision of wars between two of the four divisions of the Grecian Empire, Syria, and Egypt, which were fought over a period of about 150 years ending with Antiochus Epiphanes, who reigned about 165 B.C. Then the prophet skips over to the end time and pictures the last war between Syria and Egypt, with the result that Syria will finally overthrow Egypt. Egypt is called "the king of the south" and Syria "the king of the north" in this vision.

Daniel 11:36–12:13 definitely identifies the Antichrist as "the king of the north" (Syria) at "the time of the end." The whole purpose of the vision was to show "what shall befall thy people (Israel) in the latter days" (Dan. 10:14). The purpose of this vision over Daniel 7 and 8 is to narrow down the coming of the Antichrist geographically from the ten kingdoms of Daniel 7, and from the four kingdoms of Daniel 8 to the one kingdom of Daniel 11—the Syrian division of the old Grecian Empire—thus teaching that the Antichrist will come from Syria at the end time.

> *The Antichrist will come from one of these four divisions of Greece and will overthrow the other three, thus reviving the Grecian Empire, which will become the eighth or leopard kingdom.*

If the whole vision of Daniel 11 concerns only Egypt and Syria showing the latter–day war between them with the result that Egypt will be finally overthrown by Syria, then it proves that he will come from Syria and not Egypt, Greece or Turkey, the other three divisions of the old Grecian Empire.

"The king of the north" is the same as the "little horn" of Daniel 7 and 8, "the prince that shall come" of Daniel 9:26-27, "the son of perdition" and "man of sin" of 2 Thessalonians 2:1-12, and "the beast" of Revelation 13, as proven by the following:

1. All do according to their will for the same length of time, Dan. 7:25; 8:24; 11:36; 2 Thess. 2:10-12; Rev. 13:5-7.
2. All will exalt themselves above every god, Dan. 7:25; 8:25; 11:36-37; 2 Thess. 2:4; Rev. 13:1-18.
3. All are conquerors in the same territory at the same time, Dan. 7:8, 20-24; 8:23-25; 11:40-45; Rev. 13:1-18.
4. All speak blasphemies against God at the same time, Dan. 7:8, 11, 20-25; 8:23-25; 11:36; 2 Thess. 2:4; Rev. 13:5.
5. All prevail against the saints and Jews during the Tribulation, Dan. 7:21-26; 8:24; 11:40-41; 12:1, 7; Mt. 24:15-22; Rev. 13:1-18; 14:9-11; 15:1-4; 20:4-6.
6. All come out of the ten kingdoms of Revised Rome and get power over the ten kingdoms and reign over them until all of

them are destroyed at Armageddon, Dan. 7:7-8, 23-24; 8:9, 22-25; 11:40-45; Rev. 13:1-4; 17:9-17; 19:19-21.

7. All change the times and laws for a time, Dan. 7:11, 21-27; 8:22-25; 11:35-45; 12:7; 2 Thess. 2:1-13; Rev. 13:1-8.

8. All reign "until" the Second Coming of Christ, Dan. 2:44; 7:11-14, 18, 21-26; 8:23-25; 9:27; 11:36-45; 12:7-13; 2 Thess. 2:8-12; Rev. 17:9-17; 19:19-21.

9. All continue for the same length of time, Dan. 7:21-26; 8:22-25; 9:27; 11:40-45; 12:7-13; 2 Thess. 2:8-13; Rev. 13:5; 17:9-17; 19:19-21.

> *"The king of the north" is the same as the "little horn" of Daniel 7 and 8, "the prince that shall come" of Daniel 9:26-27, "the son of perdition" and "man of sin" of 2 Thessalonians 2:1-12, and "the beast" of Revelation 13.*

10. All will be alive when the God of Heaven comes to set up His kingdom, Dan. 2:44; 7:11-14, 18-26; 8:22-25; 9:27; 11:40-45; 12:7-13; 2 Thess. 2:8-13; Rev. 17:14; 19:19-21; 20:1-10.

11. All cause the greatest tribulation that ever will be on earth, Dan. 7:21-27; 8:19, 24-25; 9:27; 12:1, 7; Mt. 24:15-22; 2 Thess. 2:1-12; Rev. 7:14; 13:1-18; 14:9-11; 15:2-4; 20:4-6; Jer. 30:3-7.

12. All will do away with the Jewish daily sacrifices in the future temple and cause the abomination of desolation, Dan. 7:25; 8:11-14; 9:27; 11:35-45; 12:11; Mt. 24:15-22; 2 Thess. 2:4; Rev. 13:1-18.

13. All will reign in the Jewish temple in Jerusalem, Dan. 8:9-14; 9:27; 11:45; 12:7; 2 Thess. 2:4; Rev. 11:1-2; 13:1-18.

14. All will disregard the God of the fathers, Dan. 7:11, 19-25; 8:22-25; 9:27; 11:38-39; 2 Thess. 2:1-12; Jn. 5:43; Rev. 13:1-8.

15. All will honor the devil and get their power from him, Dan. 8:24; 11:35-45; 2 Thess. 2:9; Rev. 13:1-4.

16. All will come to the same end and be slain by Christ at the Second Advent and then be cast into the Lake of Fire, Dan. 2:44-45; 7:11, 21-26; 11:45; 2 Thess. 2:8-12; Rev. 19:19-21.

When Will He Come into Prominence in World Affairs?

This question is also clearly answered in Scripture:

(1) In Daniel 7:24, we have definite proof that Antichrist cannot be revealed and be prominent in world affairs, until after the ten kingdoms are formed inside the Roman Empire. According to this verse, the ten kingdoms must first be formed and exist for some time as the seventh kingdom, or Revised Rome. The Antichrist will arise and gain control over all the ten kingdoms in the first 3½ years of the Week. By the middle of the Week he will be seen as the beast of Revelation 13 coming up out of the sea of humanity already with the seven heads and ten horns, which he will have conquered before the middle of the Week. His coming

> *The Antichrist will arise and gain control over all the ten kingdoms in the first 3½ years of the Week. By the middle of the Week he will be seen as the beast of Revelation 13 coming up out of the sea of humanity already with the seven heads and ten horns.*

out of the sea in the middle of the Week will be simply the recognition of his power by the ten kingdoms and his acceptance of them from the ten kings and the dragon (Rev. 13:2-4; 17:12-17). This verse further teaches that, because of his rise out of the ten kingdoms, he is to come out of obscurity and that his rise to power will be quick. Daniel saw the "little horn" rising so suddenly among the ten that he was bewildered (Dan. 7:7-8, 19-24). Therefore, no man can determine who the Antichrist will be until after the ten kingdoms are formed.

(2) The Antichrist cannot be revealed until the rapture as proved in the following passage:

> And now ye know what withholdeth that he might be revealed in his time. For the mystery of iniquity doth already work: only he who now letteth will let, until he be taken out of the way.
>
> And then shall that Wicked be revealed, whom the Lord shall consume with the spirit of his

mouth, and shall destroy with the brightness of his coming (2 Thess. 2:6-8)

How Long is His Reign?

He will reign over one of the ten kingdoms of Revised Rome at the beginning of the Week and will obtain control over the whole ten kingdoms during the last 3½ years (Rev. 13: 5; 7:25; 12:7). It is in these last 3½ years that he will exalt himself above every God and will be worshipped by many of his subjects (Rev. 13:14-18; Dan. 8: 25; 11:36-45; 2 Thess. 2:4).

> *Daniel saw the "little horn" rising so suddenly among the ten that he was bewildered (Dan. 7:7-8, 19-24). Therefore, no man can determine who the Antichrist will be until after the ten kingdoms are formed.*

Where is He to Reign?

During part of the last 3½ years he will reign in Jerusalem "in the glorious holy mountain" where the temple will be rebuilt (Dan. 11:45). He will sit "in the temple of God, showing himself that he is God" (2 Thess. 2:4). This temple is where the abomination of desolation will be placed (Dan. 9: 27; 12:7-13; Mt. 24:15-22; Rev. 11:1-2; 13: 12-18). Babylon, and not Rome, will be his place of reign until then.

The fact that there will be ten separate kingdoms with ten separate capitals and ten separate kings in the first 3½ years shows that up to the middle of the Week the Antichrist does not have one capitol where he reigns over the ten kingdoms, for they will not yet be under his control. Rome will be just one of the ten capitals and her king will reign over the territory of Italy and her possessions and not over all of Revised Rome. It is only when Antichrist becomes head of the ten kingdoms by the middle of the Week that he will establish one central throne in Jerusalem for all the newly formed empire. Even then, the kings will continue to rule under him (Rev. 17:9-17).

The Power of the Antichrist

The power of the Antichrist will come from Satan, the spirit of the Abyss, and the ten kings. His power has already been predicted by God and it will be given him in due time. It is God who will permit Satan and his agents to give their power to the Beast and inspire him in his evil designs (Dan. 8:24; 2 Thess. 2:8-12; Rev. 13: 1-2). It is God who will put it into the hearts of the ten kings to give him their power for the purpose of destroying Mystical Babylon (Rev. 17:12-17). It is the satanic prince out of the Abyss (Rev. 11: 7; 17:8) who will be the executive of Satan's power to the Beast and who will inspire and back the Antichrist in all his diabolical activities. Satan will give to the Antichrist the world–kingdoms he offered Christ. Antichrist will accept them; Christ did not.

> *The power of the Antichrist will come from Satan, the spirit of the Abyss, and the ten kings. His power has already been predicted by God and it will be given him in due time.*

The Antichrist must fight to possess them even as Christ would have had to do and will yet have to do. Antichrist will succeed in this world conquest by conquering the Revised Roman Empire by the middle of the Week and all the northern and eastern countries of Asia and Europe by the end of the Week. Also he will obtain the co–operation of many other nations through the ministry of the three unclean spirits, who will help him fight against the Jews and Christ at the Second Advent. After his defeat at Armageddon by Christ, the Antichrist will be cast into the Lake of Fire. The kingdom of God will succeed his kingdom and extend throughout all the earth. The power of the Beast may be summarized as follows:

1. To blaspheme God (Dan. 7:8, 11, 20, 25; 11:36; Rev. 13:5-6).
2. To overcome saints (Rev. 7:9-17; 14: 13; 15:2-4).
3. To overcome the Jews (Dan. 7:21; 12:7; Rev. 13:7, 15).
4. To conquer many nations (Dan. 7:8, 20-24; 11:36-45; Ezek. 38–39) and rule

them as he wills (Rev. 13:7).

5. To destroy Mystery Babylon (Rev. 17: 12-17).

6. To overcome and kill the two witnesses (Rev. 11:7).

7. To change times and laws (Dan. 7:25).

8. To understand mysteries (Dan. 8:23).

9. To protect the Jews as long as he desires, and also to succeed in destroying them for a period (Dan. 9:27; 2 Thess. 2:4; Rev. 11:1-2).

10. To work signs and wonders (Dan. 8:24; 2 Thess. 2:8-12; Rev. 13:1-18; 19:20).

11. To cause craft to prosper (Dan. 8:25).

12. To control money and riches in his own realm (Dan. 11:38-43).

13. To cause great deceptions (2 Thess. 2:10-12; Jn. 5:43; Dan. 8:25; Rev. 13:1-18).

14. To do according to his own will (Dan. 11:36).

15. To control religion and worship (Dan 11:36; 2 Thess. 2:4; Rev. 13:1-18; 14: 9-11; 16:21).

16. To control the lives of all men in his realm (Rev. 13:12-18).

17. To control kings as he wills (Rev. 17: 12-17).
18. To make all the other nations fear him (Rev. 13:4).
19. To fight against Christ (Rev. 19:11-21; Dan. 8:25).
20. To reign forty–two months (Rev. 13:5).

His Person

The Antichrist will be a real person and not a religious system or the successive head of a religious system, such as the pope. He is yet to come to power in the future and will literally fulfill all the prophecies concerning himself. His character and characteristics are clearly implied in the points above, which reveal that he will be a man who will possess the talent and leadership qualities found in all gifted conquerors and leaders. In addition to these natural gifts, he will possess the miraculous power of attracting people of every class, fascinating them with his marvelous personality, successes, wisdom, administrative and executive ability, bringing them under his control through his well-directed flattery and masterly diplomacy. He will be indued with the power of Satan in the exercise of these gifts until the world will wonder after him and many will worship him as God.

Chapter Four

EVENTS FOLLOWING THE BATTLE OF ARMAGEDDON

THE EXPULSION OF SATAN FROM THE EARTH

And I saw an angel come down from heaven, having the key of the bottomless pit and a great chain in his hand. And he laid hold on the dragon, that old serpent, which is the Devil, and Satan, and bound him a thousand years. And cast him into the bottomless pit, and shut him up, and set a seal upon him, that he should deceive the nations no more, till the thousand years should be fulfilled: and after that he must be loosed a little season (Rev. 20:1-3)

This passage is the continuation of the

scripture on the Battle of Armageddon of Revelation 19:11-21 and shows the confinement of the Dragon in the Abyss. After Armageddon, an angel will come down from Heaven having the key to the Abyss. How an angel or a spirit can be bound by a literal chain and be cast into a material place is only understandable when we see that angels can be localized and confined to material places. If this is not true, how are demons that are now bound in this Abyss to be loosed under the fifth and sixth trumpets? How can angels be confined to Tartarus in chains (2 Pet. 2:4; Jude 6-7) and how will all wicked men, demons, fallen angels, and rebellious creatures of all kinds be confined in the Lake of Fire forever? (Mt. 25:41; Rev. 14:9-11; 19:20; 20:10-15).

> *After Armageddon, an angel will come down from Heaven having the key to the Abyss. How an angel or a spirit can be bound by a literal chain and be cast into a material place is only understandable when we see that angels can be localized and confined to material places.*

This angel mentioned in Revelation 20:

1-3 will lay hold on Satan, overpower him by actual combat, bind him with a great chain, cast him into the Abyss where he will be for a thousand years and "set a seal upon him," or literally, seal the Abyss over him to keep him there so that he cannot deceive the nations until the Millennium is over. Thus we see that Satan is a literal person, his doom is literal, he is to be bound by a literal angel, with a literal chain, cast into a literal Abyss, and sealed with a literal seal for the period of the Millennium.

In Revelation 12 we have seen that the Dragon and his angels will be cast out of Heaven to the earth in the middle of the Week, where they will remain until the Battle of Armageddon when they will fight against Christ and His angels and saints. It is not stated whether Satan's angels will be cast into the Abyss with him or not. In Isaiah 24: 21-22; 25:7 it is clear that they will be cast into the pit with Satan and will be loosed with him "After many days" to help him deceive the nations again (Rev. 20:1-10).

Chapter Five

THE BOOK OF REVELATION

The Three Divisions of Revelation

1. "Write the things which thou hast seen" (Rev. 1:19). That is, as the first division of this book write the vision that you saw of me (Christ) in the midst of the candlesticks in Rev. 1:11-18. This John did in the first chapter of the book.

2. "Write the things which are" (Rev. 1:19). That is, in the second division of the book of Revelation write the things that I (Christ) will tell you to write about concerning the churches, or concerning the Church on earth. This John did in Rev. 2:1–3:22.

3. "Write the things which must be hereafter" (Rev. 1:19). That is, as the third and last division of the book of Revelation write the things that I (Christ) will show you after you have completed things concerning

the churches. These last things do not concern the things of the churches—they concern events after the church age. These things to happen after the church age were recorded by John in Revelation 4:1–22:21.

The Key to the Book of Revelation

If one will accept this simple threefold division of Revelation, as in the above, and keep every detail of the events in the proper division as revealed, this will truly serve as the key to an understanding of the entire book. All that is required for an understanding of these events is to take them literally as things to happen on the earth from John's day forward into all eternity to come, making sure above all else that each event is put in its proper place or order of events as they are revealed—each in its own division, not mixing those things concerning the Church with those things which must be after the churches.

We have in the things concerning the

churches, and the events which must be after the churches two separate and distinct series of happenings that cover two separate and distinct periods of time—one period covering the church age (Rev. 2:1–3:22), and the other covering the time from the end of the church period, or church age, into all eternity to come (Rev. 4:1–22:5). Whenever we see that "the things which are" belong to the church age, and that "the things which must be after the things which are" belong to the period from the close of the church age on into all eternity, then the entire book becomes as simple to understand as John 3:16. The main thing to keep in mind is that Revelation 4:1–22:21 will be fulfilled after the church age, and, therefore, after the rapture of the Church. Not one of these latter–day details has anything to do with the church age.

Appendix

BIBLICAL STUDIES

I. THE BIBLE IS EASY TO UNDERSTAND

The Bible is a simple book to understand. We've seen that as we've studied a topic that many consider complex and obscure. Even biblical prophecy, an area of Scripture that many assume to be beyond comprehension, is as easy to understand as the accounts of Jonah, Daniel or Joseph. This probably sounds ridiculous to most people, but perhaps considering a few simple facts will change your mind! Consider the following points:

The Bible is a Revelation. The Bible is an inspired revelation from God. A revelation is an uncovering or unveiling so that everyone may see what was previously covered or hidden.

The Bible Contains Many Repeated Truths. Over and over the Bible repeats truth so that "in the mouth of two or three witnesses every word may be established" (Dt. 17:6-7; 19:15; Mt. 18:16; 2 Cor. 13:1; 1 Tim. 5:19; Heb. 10:28). Because of this fact, any doctrine that is not plainly stated in Scripture is best left alone. When God says something about a particular topic, it will be found repeated in several places, so we will not be left in doubt as to what God says. Our part is to collect everything God says on a subject—making it so clear that no interpretation is necessary. If we do this, nothing will need to be added to or taken from the Bible in order to understand the truth. All we need to do is to find out where "it is written" and then believe it. We must always make our ideas conform to the Bible and not the Scripture to our ideas.

> *Because of this fact, any doctrine that is not plainly stated in Scripture is best left alone. When God says something about a particular topic, it will be found repeated in several places, so we will not be left in doubt as to what God says.*

The Bible is Written in Simple Language. It is intended to be read and understood without interpretation. All God considers necessary to understand the Bible is child-like faith. God made both man and His Word, and they fit together as a lock and key (Job 32:8; 38:3-6; Jn. 1:4-9). Even the ungodly can understand, if they so desire (Rom. 1:16-20).

The Bible is a Simple Book to Understand Because Most of it is Either History or Simple Instructions About How to Live. About 25,007 verses of the Bible—about 80 percent of it—contain simple history, commands, warnings, promises, rebukes, and plain instructions by means of which men may understand the will of God. The remaining 20 percent (or 6,207 verses) are prophecy written in the same simple human language that is used to record history. Of these 6,207 prophetic verses, 3,299 have been fulfilled and are now history. The 2,908 other verses are unfulfilled prophecy.

II. DEFINITION OF TERMS

It is important to define some of the important terms we'll be using in this book:

INTERPRET: To state the true sense of God's message as He expresses it; that is, give to the reader the exact statements of Scripture without change; to state exactly what God says and where He says it.

HERMENEUTICS is the science or art of interpretation and explanation. It comes from the Greek *hermeneuo*, meaning "to explain," "to expound," and "to interpret" (Jn. 1:38-42; 9:7; Heb. 7:2). It is the science which establishes and classifies the principles, methods and rules by which the meaning of the author's language is ascertained. The interpretation of any piece of literature will depend upon the nature of the work under consideration. Poetry, history, fiction, and other forms of human expression require a different set of rules. The rules that govern the writing of fiction would not be suitable for historical prose. Accordingly, the rules that govern biblical interpretation depend upon the character of its separate kinds of writings, just as is true of different kinds of writings in other books.

Since the Bible is like other books in that it is written in human language, it must be interpreted like all other literature. If heavenly, supernatural, and spiritual truths are written in human language, we must understand such truths on this basis. The words and expressions found in the Bible must be understood in the same manner as words and expressions found outside of it. There can be no special biblical logic, rhetoric, or grammar. The laws of grammar apply to the Bible as they do to other writings.

BIBLICAL HERMENEUTICS is the science which establishes and classifies the principles, methods, and rules by which the Word of God is made plain.

EXEGESIS is the application of the rules of biblical hermeneutics to the unfolding of the meaning of a passage of Scripture. Interpretation expresses exactly the mind and thoughts of another and is purely a reproductive process, involving no originality of thought on the part of the interpreter. Exegesis is the use of the science of interpretation in the reproduction of the thoughts of God as expressed in Scripture.

III. THE TRUE METHOD OF BIBLE INTERPRETATION

The fundamental principle is to gather from the Scriptures themselves the precise meaning the writers intended to convey. It applies to the Bible the same principles, rules, grammatical process, and exercise of common sense and reason that we apply to other books. In doing this, one must take the Bible as literal when it is at all possible. When a statement is found that cannot possibly be literal, as Jesus being a "door" or of a woman being clothed with the sun and standing on the moon and on her head a crown of twelve stars, or of land animals coming out of the sea, and other statements which are obviously not literal, then we know the language is figurative. In such cases

80

we must get the literal truth conveyed by the figurative language, and the truth intended to be conveyed will be as literal as if it were expressed in literal language without the use of such figures. After all, figurative language expresses literal truth as much as if such figures were not used. In a general sense, the true method of Bible interpretation embraces the following ideas:

> *The fundamental principle is to gather from the Scriptures themselves the precise meaning the writers intended to convey. It applies to the Bible the same principles, rules, grammatical process, and exercise of common sense and reason that we apply to other books.*

1. The primary meaning of words and their common use in a particular age in which they are used, and the importance of synonyms.
2. The grammatical construction and idiomatic peculiarities of the languages of the Bible, and the meaning of the context, both immediate and remote.
3. Comparison of parallel passages on the same subject.

4. The purpose or object of each writer in each particular book.
5. The historical background of each writer and the circumstances under which he wrote.
6. The general plan of the entire Bible, and its moral and spiritual teachings.
7. The agreement of the various subjects found in Scripture, and the corresponding prophecies and their fulfillment.

> *When all these facts are kept in mind and all scriptures interpreted in harmony with these principles, there won't be any misunderstanding of any part of the Bible.*

8. The manners and customs of the particular age and land of each writer.
9. Understanding of how to interpret prophecy, poetry, allegories, symbols, parables, figures of speech, types and all other forms of human expression.

When all these facts are kept in mind by the student and all Scripture interpreted in harmony with all these principles, there cannot possibly be any misunderstanding of any part of the Bible.

IV. GENERAL RULES OF BIBLE INTERPRETATION

1. The entire Bible came from God and possesses unity of design and teaching. We shall, therefore, consider both Testaments together as being equally inspired.

2. It may be assumed that no one resorts to speech or writing without having some idea to express; that in order to express that idea he will use words and forms of speech familiar to his hearers or readers; and that if he uses a word or figure of speech in a different sense from what is commonly understood he will make the fact known.

3. The Bible cannot contradict itself. Its teachings in one part must agree with its teachings in another part. Therefore, any interpretation which makes the Bible inconsistent with itself must rest upon false principles.

4. No meaning should be gotten from the Bible except that which a fair and honest, grammatical, and historical interpretation yields.

5. Language is an accumulation of words used to interchange thoughts. To understand the language of the speaker or writer, it is necessary to know the meaning of his words. A true meaning of the words is a true meaning of the sense. It is as true of the Bible as of any other book.

6. Often to fully understand a passage of Scripture, the scope or plan of the entire book must be known. Sometimes the design of the books are made clear, as in the case of Proverbs (1:1-4), Isaiah (1:1-3), John (20:31), and Revelation (1:1). If the definite purpose of the book is not stated, the purpose of the book must be gotten from the contents and from the design of the Bible as a whole, as is clear in John 5:39; 2 Timothy

> *Some seeming contradictions are cleared up when this rule is observed. The difference between Paul and James is easily understood when the design of their books is understood and recognized. In Romans, Paul seeks to prove that a man is not saved by works, while in James he seeks to show that a man cannot remain saved unless he brings forth good works.*

2:15; 3:16-17. Some seeming contradictions are cleared up when this rule is observed. The difference between Paul and James is easily understood when the design of their books is understood and recognized. In Romans, Paul seeks to prove that a man is not saved by works, while in James he seeks to show that a man cannot remain saved unless he brings forth good works.

7.   Sometimes the connection is obscured through the use of virtual dialogue between the writers and unseen persons, as in Ps. 15; Isa. 52:13; 63:1-6 and Rom. 3.

8.   One of the most fundamental rules of interpretation is that of comparing scripture with scripture. It is by a strict and honest observance of this rule that the true meaning can be gotten when every other thing has failed to make clear the meaning. Before arriving at the whole truth, be sure that all the scriptures on a subject are collected together and read at one time. If there is any question left after you have done this, then go over the whole subject carefully until every question is cleared up.

9.   In some places a statement on a subject may be very brief and seemingly obscure and will be made perfectly clear by a larger passage on the same subject. Always explain the seemingly difficult with the more simple scriptures. No doctrine founded upon a single verse of Scripture contains the whole of the subject; so do not be dishonest and wrest with Scripture or force a meaning into a passage that is not clearly understood in the passage or in parallel passages on the same subject.

10.   The progressive character of revelation and the gradual development of truth should be recognized. Some truths found in germ in the Old Testament are fully developed in the New Testament. For example, the idea of blood sacrifices was developed from the time of Abel until it was fully culminated and made eternally clear in the sacrifice of Christ on Calvary.

11.   The meaning of a word or phrase in the New Testament must not be carried back into Old Testament doctrine unless such is

warranted by both Testaments. For example, water baptism, the Lord's Supper, and other New Testament doctrines are not found in the Old Testament at all. It is not proper to ask whether David was baptized in water, or whether Saul was a Christian, because these are New Testament terms.

12. Passages obviously literal should not be spiritualized. For example, making the natural blessings of Canaan the spiritual blessings of Heaven; regarding the ark of Noah as salvation through Christ, and hundreds of like interpretations.

13. The dispensational character of Scripture should be noted so that one can pigeonhole every passage of Scripture in some definite period in God's plan.

14. The three classes of people (the Jews, the Church, and the Gentiles) dealt with in Scripture should be noted. Up to Genesis 12, the race as a whole is dealt with. From Gen. 12 to the New Testament the Jews and the Gentiles are dealt with; and in the New Testament these and the Church of God,

made up of Jews and Gentiles, are dealt with (1 Cor. 10:32).

15. In all study of doctrine the practical aspect must be kept in view (2 Tim. 3:16-17).

16. The comparative importance of truth should be emphasized. The positive truths should be studied more than the negative. It is more important to have faith instead of unbelief; to know God better than Satan, etc. So one should learn more about faith and God than unbelief and Satan.

17. General familiarity with the Bible as a whole is very important. Keep reading the Bible over and over until its contents as a whole are familiar. The more one can remember here and there what he has read, the clearer the Bible will become.

18. Words of Scripture must agree with the content and the subject matter in the passages where found. No meaning should be given to a word that would be in the least out of harmony with any Scripture. For example, the word "seen" in John 1:18 should be

understood to mean "comprehended" in order to harmonize with all scriptures that state men saw God with the natural eyes.

19. Careful attention should be paid to connecting words that connect events with each other, as the words "when," "then," etc., in Mt. 24:15-16, 21, 23, 40; 25:1.

20. Careful attention should be paid to prepositions, definite articles, names of different persons and places with the same name, same persons and places with different names, and the names of different persons and places that are spelled differently by different authors in different books.

21. Ascertain the exact meaning of the words of Scripture. The way a word is used, the subject matter, and the context often determine the true meaning.

22. Hebrew and Greek idioms should be noted. Sometimes a person having a peculiar characteristic, or subject to a peculiar evil, or destined to a particular destiny is called the child of that evil or destiny (Lk. 10:6; Eph.

2:1-3; 2 Thess. 2:3). The word "father" is applied to the originator of any custom or to the inventor of something (Gen. 4:20-21; Jn. 8:44). It is also used for ancestor (1 Chr. 1:17). The words "son" and "daughter" are sometimes used of descendants or in–laws. (Gen. 46:22; Lk. 3:23). The words "brother" and "cousin" are sometimes used of relatives and countrymen (Gen. 14:16 with 11:31; Lk. 1:36, 58). Names of parents are used of posterity (1 Ki. 18:17-18).

23. Preference is sometimes expressed by the word "hate" (Lk. 14:26; Rom. 9:13).

24. A peculiar idiom concerning numbers must be understood. Sometimes round numbers rather than the exact number are used (Judg. 20:35, 46). This will explain seeming contradictions between numbers. Failure to understand this idiom may have caused copyists and translators to misunderstand the numbers of some passages which seem erroneous and very large. For example, in 1 Sam. 6:19, we read the Lord smote in a very small town 50,070 people, which, in the Hebrew

text reads, "seventy men two fifties and one thousand" or 70–100–1,000, or 1,170 people.

25. Careful attention should be paid to parenthesis, the use of italics (meaning these words are not in the original but supplied in English to make sense), the use of capital letters, marginal notes, references, summaries of chapters, chapter and page headings, the division of the text into chapters and verses, punctuation, obsolete English words, the rendering of the same original words by different English words, and other things about the English translations. All these things are human additions to the original text and should not be relied upon. For example, the running of references to prove a doctrine is sometimes misleading. The references may not be on the same subject, as can be easily detected by the reader.

26. Seeming contradictions in Scripture should be considered in the light of all the principles stated above. It must be kept in mind that the Bible records sayings of men

under pressure of trials who said things that they never would have said otherwise. It records sayings of backsliders and rebels against God. It records statements of Satan and demons, and the words of such rebels should never be taken as the words from the mouth of God. They should not always be held as truth, for sometimes they are lies. Inspiration guarantees that these rebels said those things, but it does not guarantee that what they said is truth. Sometimes such statements contradict those of God and good men under divine utterance. Enemies of God take such contradictions between what God says and what rebels against God say and use them to prove the Bible contradicts itself. Naturally, such contradictions are found in the Bible, but they are not contradictions between statements made by God. The only statements that can be relied upon as truth are those that come from God and men who speak for God as the Spirit gives utterance, and in these there is no contradiction.

The Bible also records the changes of God's will and plan in a later age over that of an earlier one. Such changes have been taken by the ungodly as contradictions, but such have had to be made by God because of the sin and rebellion of the people to whom He promised such things and for whom He made a certain plan. For example, in Gen. 1:31 God saw everything that He had made and it was good, but in Gen. 6:6 God repented that He had made man. In the meantime, between the two passages, sin and rebellion had entered, which made it necessary for God to have a changed attitude toward man. God has had to change his plan temporarily because of man's sin, but the original and eternal plan of God for creation has never been changed and never will be. God will finally realize His original purpose; that is the reason for His present dispensational dealings. God deals with each generation as circumstances demand. Sometimes God has had to change His promises to a certain group because they refused to meet the conditions for the fulfillment of these promises.

27. The seeming contradictions in the New Testament will also vanish and will be

cleared up if men would be as fair with God as they will want God to be with them in the judgment. Always look for an explanation and it will be found. For example, men criticize the Bible for lack of harmony between the temptations of Christ in Mt. 4, and those in Lk. 4. But when we consider the fact that there were two separate sets of temptations during the forty days, and that after the first set of tests in Luke, Satan was dismissed "for a season," and after the last set of tests in Matthew, Satan was dismissed for good, there is no contradiction. The seeming contradictions between the sermons of Mt. 5 and Lk. 6 are cleared up when we see that there were two sermons—one on the mount and the other "in the plain." The so-called contradictions of the Bible are unreal and imaginary. Because of the lack of information as to the time, places, circumstances, etc., men cannot always judge concerning them. So it would be best always to give God the benefit of the doubt, since He knows all things and was there when things happened. If He did not see fit to give all details so as to make every small detail clear, that is His wisdom. It should not detract from faith in God and His revelation.

All seeming contradictions in the Bible are easily cleared up with a better knowledge of the text, by correct translation, by knowing the manners and customs of the age and the country in which the books were written, by a wider application of historical facts, and by a fair and sane application of the rules of interpretation given above.

NOTES